Becoming Kobe Bryant

written by Ahmad K Smith

This book Belongs to:

To all the children who love sports

Kobe Bryant was born in Philadelphia and started playing basketball at the age of three. He grew up a Lakers fan, which was his favorite team.

His father played for the 76ers and overseas Kobe grew up in Italy and would come back to the states and play in summer leagues.

Kobe learned three styles of play. The International, American, and Streetball style, all helped his game.

He blended all three to become the first freshman to start on the Lower Merion High School varsity team, at the age of thirteen.

Kobe became a high school legend and had college offers from Duke and UNC, but Kobe skipped college to go straight to the league. It was clear that Kobe was a basketball prodigy.

At first, people didn't know what to expect. But in Kobe's rookie season, he silenced the doubt by winning the dunk contest.

By his 4th season, he was already the best guard in the league. He would go on to 3 peat with Shaq as they became the best duo in NBA history.

Kobe's style of play was similar to his idol Michael Jordan, Kobe wore number eight and had the same mentality of destroying his opponents.

He even dropped 81 points in one single game. Which is second all-time in the history of the NBA.

81 POINTS

10

After ten seasons, he changed his number from 8 to 24 and gave the game a new meaning. Number eight Kobe was more youthful and athletic, twenty-four Kobe was more advanced and seasoned.

Kobe became the most skilled player ever to play. He was smooth, fierce, and had a competitive fire in his DNA.

Kobe's nickname was the Black Mamba because of his hard work, dedication, and passion. The mamba mentality was birthed and will never go out of fashion.

He won an MVP and two championships wearing the number twenty-four jersey. Winning a total of five championships in his NBA journey.

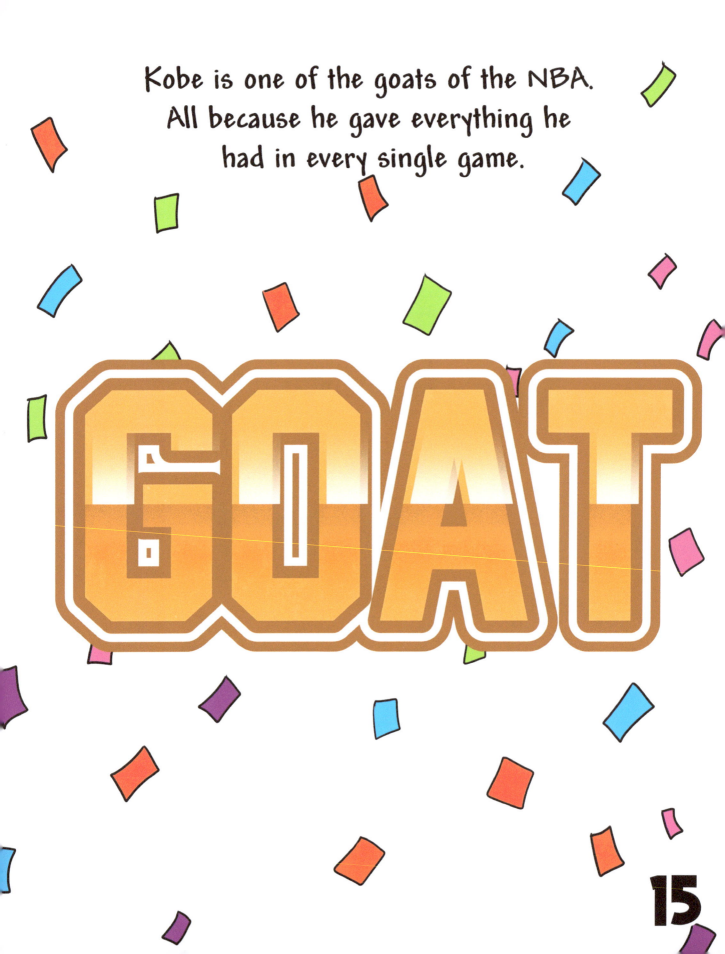

Kobe is one of the goats of the NBA. All because he gave everything he had in every single game.

GOAT

When he retired he won an Oscar award for creating the best short animation film. Kobe was still winning even outside of the basketball realm.

Unfortunately, his life was cut short due to a helicopter crash. Along with his daughter and seven others. The sadness is still hard to pass.

- KOBE BRYANT - GIANA BRYANT
- JHON ALTOBELLI - ALYSSA ALTOBELLLI
- KERI ALTOBELLY - CHRISTINA MAUSER
- SARAH CHESTER - PAYTON CHESTER
- ARA ZOBAYAN

Kobe inspired the world and changed countless lives his presence will live forever and his greatness will never die.

The End

Ahmad K Smith was born and raised in Saint Louis, Missouri. Growing up he had a love for basketball and storytelling. Later Ahmad channeled both passions into a career in sports media broadcasting and marketing. Ahmad is thankful to his family and friends who helped him along the way and intends to open doors for the next generation behind him.

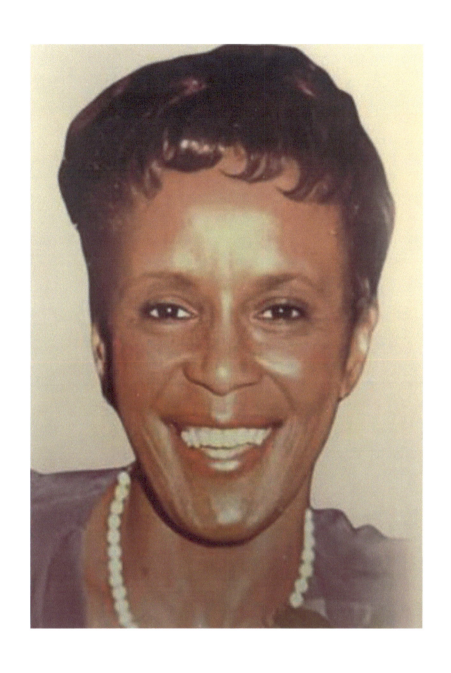

"In loving memory of my grandma, whose warmth and wisdom continue to light my path every day. Your love is forever cherished."

Printed in the USA
CPSIA information can be obtained
at www.ICGtesting.com
CBHW040738061024
15371CB00011B/116